This is one of a series of books on modern art designed to help very young people learn the basic vocabulary used by artists, a sort of ABC of art. Parents and teachers play a key role in this learning process, encouraging careful, thoughtful looking. This book isolates lines to show how they are used by artists and how they contribute to meaning in art. By looking at lines and discussing what thoughts and feelings they convey, adults encourage children to develop creative thinking skills. At the back of this book, there is more information about the pictures included to help in this engaging process.

Enjoy looking together!

Lines

Philip Yenawine

[handwritten inscription: To ... To ... & her kids! Best wishes!]

The Museum of Modern Art, New York
Delacorte Press

Acknowledgements
This book was made possible by the generosity of The Eugene and Estelle Ferkauf Foundation; John and Margot Ernst; David Rockefeller, Jr.; John and Jodie Eastman; Joan Ganz Cooney; and The Astrid Johansen Memorial Gift Fund. Of equal importance were the talents of Takaaki Matsumoto, Michael McGinn, Mikio Sakai, David Gale, Harriet Bee, Richard Tooke, Mikki Carpenter, Nancy Miller, Alexander Gray, Carlos Silveira, and particularly Catherine Grimshaw. I am extremely grateful to all of them.

Library of Congress Cataloging in Publication Data

Yenawine, Philip.
Lines/by Philip Yenawine.
        p.   cm.
Summary: Isolates the artistic element of lines, discusses what thoughts and feelings can be conveyed by different lines, and examines how they contribute to a work of art through various examples.
ISBN 0-385-30253-3 (trade ed.). –ISBN 0-385-30313-0 (lib. ed.)
1. Line (Art)–Juvenile literature.   [1. Line (Art)   2. Art appreciation.]
I. Title
NC754.Y46 1991
760′.01–dc20   90–38283   CIP   AC

ISBN 0-87070-175-4 (MoMA)

The Museum of Modern Art
11 West 53 Street
New York, NY 10019

Delacorte Press
Bantam Doubleday Dell Publishing Group, Inc.
1540 Broadway
New York, New York 10036

Printed in Italy

May 1991

10 9 8 7 6 5 4 3 2

Artists make pictures out of lines.

Pablo Picasso, *The Kitchen*

1

Lines start with a dot •
And a dot grows into a line ••••••••••••
And from there to a whole picture made of dots and lines.

Vincent van Gogh, *Street at Saintes-Maries*

Here's a picture made only from lines crossing over one another.
Look very carefully.

Giorgio Morandi, *Still Life with Coffeepot*

Some lines are straight. ———————

Some curve.

Some zigzag.

Some loop.

Some make shapes.

Can you find curving lines and straight ones, loops and zigzags?
What shapes can you find?

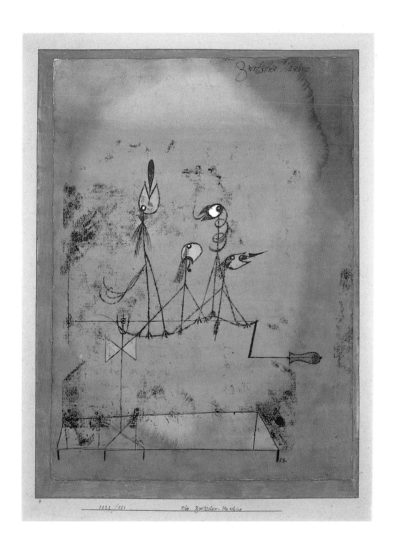

Paul Klee, *Twittering Machine*

Of course, lines can be any color.

Franz Marc, *Blue Horse with Rainbow*

And there are many ways to make them.

Brushes   Pens   Crayons   Pencils   Fingers

Some lines are thin.

Henri Matisse, *The Swan*, plate 24 from *Poésies* by Stéphane Mallarmé

Some are thick.

Georgia O'Keeffe, *Evening Star, III*

9

Lines can sparkle and wiggle.

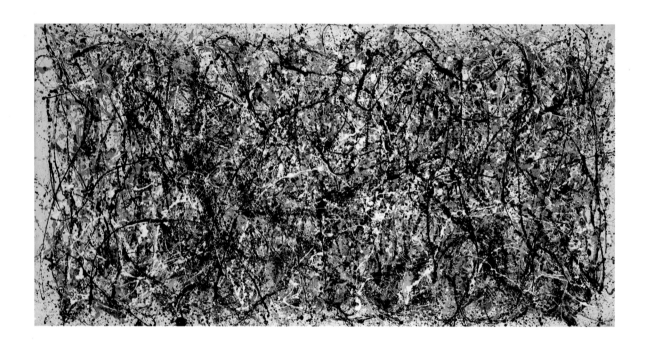

Jackson Pollock, *One (Number 31, 1950)*

Detail of Pollock, *One (Number 31, 1950)*

Lines can help us imagine things.

Vasily Kandinsky, *Watercolor (Number 13)*

Can you imagine clouds?

A boat?

Smoke?

Can you find a line moving fast?

Moving slowly?

What else can you find?

Artists draw what they see.

Theo van Doesburg (C. E. M. Küpper), Two Studies for *Composition (The Cow)*

14

But then they can change things. Do you see how the cow changes?

Theo van Doesburg (C. E. M. Küpper), Two Studies for *Composition (The Cow)*

15

Artists draw outlines of shapes we know. Find people and pictures and plants and chairs.

Henri Matisse, *The Red Studio*

But not all the lines outline shapes.
How many other places can you see lines?

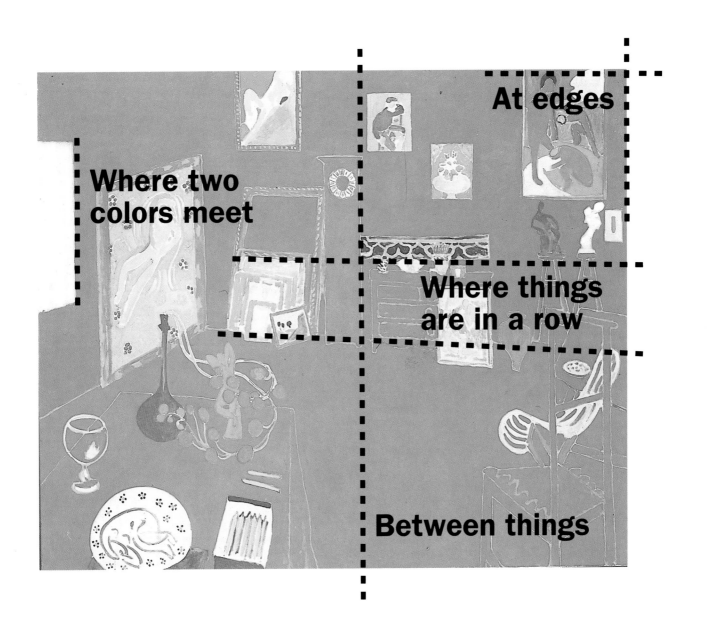

At edges

Where two colors meet

Where things are in a row

Between things

This picture has lines that you will find if you look carefully.

André Derain, *London Bridge*

Can you find:

A line of yellow light flashing on the green water?

Lines of swirling water beneath the bridge?

A line of traffic on the bridge?

How do you think you would feel walking across this bridge?

This painting is made up of tiny lines of color.

Vincent van Gogh, *The Starry Night*

Lines make all sorts of shapes. Find these:

They tell a story about a very bright and starry night in a small village. Can you tell the rest of the story?

Can you draw a picture with thick lines and thin lines, with curves and colors, with shapes we know? With lines to make us imagine?

The art in this book can be found at The Museum of Modern Art in New York City. Other museums and galleries have many interesting pictures too, and it is good to make a habit of visiting them, looking for lines. You can also look in magazines, books, buildings, parks, and gardens.

Page 1

Page 2

Pablo Picasso
The Kitchen, 1948
Oil on canvas
69" x 8' 2 1/2" (175 x 250 cm)
Acquired through the Nelson A. Rockefeller Bequest

Widely admired for inventing new systems for composing pictures, Picasso never abandoned images that relate, somehow, to the real world. This is an abstracted representation of Picasso's kitchen as seen from his studio window.

Vincent van Gogh
Street at Saintes-Maries, 1888
Brush, reed pen and ink, and traces of pencil on paper
9 5/8 x 12 1/2" (24.5 x 31.8 cm)
Abby Aldrich Rockefeller Bequest

Part of the emotional power of van Gogh's work comes from the use of short, choppy strokes, which can also be seen in *The Starry Night,* this book's final image.

Page 3

Page 5

Page 6

Page 8

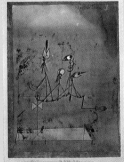

Giorgio Morandi
Still Life with Coffeepot, 1933
Etching
11 11/16 x 15 3/8" (29.7 x 39 cm)
Mrs. Bertram Smith Fund

The quiet, timeless quality in this still life by Morandi derives partly from the slow, painstaking construction of images by cross-hatching lines.

Paul Klee
Twittering Machine, 1922
Watercolor and pen and ink on oil transfer drawing on paper, mounted on cardboard
25 1/4 x 19" (mounted)
(63.8 x 48.1 cm)
Purchase

Klee's work is valued in part for his playful images and his equally free use of materials and techniques. Children are likely to be amused by the thought of Klee's funny "birds" twittering while they work.

Franz Marc
Blue Horse with Rainbow, 1913
Watercolor, gouache, and pencil on paper
6 3/8 x 10 1/8" (16.2 x 25.7 cm)
John S. Newberry Collection

Franz Marc sought expression of the spirit through colors and the use of the horse as a symbol of freedom and strength.

Henri Matisse
The Swan, plate 24 from *Poésies* by Stéphane Mallarmé
Lausanne, Skira, 1932
Etching
Page 13 x 9 3/4" (33 x 24.7 cm)
Louis E. Stern Collection

Always striving to perfect his drawing skills, Matisse developed the capacity to describe objects with a sure and simple line while also maintaining an eye for overall design.

Page 9

Georgia O'Keeffe
Evening Star, III 1917
Watercolor on paper
9 x 11 7/8" (22.7 x 30.2 cm)
Mr. and Mrs. Donald B. Straus Fund

O'Keeffe specialized in looking
closely at nature and representing
its phenomena—such as sunsets—
somewhat abstractly and rich in
color.

Page 10

Jackson Pollock
One (Number 31, 1950), 1950
Oil and enamel paint on canvas
8' 10" x 17' 5 5/8" (269.5 x 530.8 cm)
Sidney and Harriet Janis Collection
Fund (by exchange)

Pollock's painting technique
replaced careful brushwork with
athletic action. He poured, dripped,
and cast huge networks of lines and
colors that flickered with light,
encapsulating the energy of America
at midcentury.

Page 12

Vasily Kandinsky
Watercolor (Number 13), 1913
Watercolor on paper
12 5/8 x 16 1/8" (32.1 x 41 cm)
Katherine S. Dreier Bequest

Kandinsky was interested in convey-
ing the spiritual side of nature by
representing it in organic rhythms of
line and color.

Page 14

Theo van Doesburg
(C. E. M. Küpper)
Study for *Composition (The Cow)*,
c. 1917
Pencil on paper
Sheet 4 5/8 x 6 1/4" (11.8 x 17.1 cm)
Purchase

Simplifying is an aspect of abstrac-
tion, and here van Doesburg
reduced a drawing of an actual cow
into geometric shapes, finally
depicting the idea of a cow, stolid
and blocky.

Page 14

Theo van Doesburg
(C. E. M. Küpper)
Study for *Composition (The Cow)*,
c. 1917
Pencil on paper
Sheet 4 1/8 x 5 3/4" (10.4 x 14.6 cm)
Gift of Nelly van Doesburg

Page 15

Theo van Doesburg
(C. E. M. Küpper)
Study for *Composition (The Cow)*,
c. 1917
Pencil on paper
Sheet 4 5/8 x 6 1/4" (11.8 x 17.1 cm)
Purchase

Page 15

Theo van Doesburg
(C. E. M. Küpper)
Study for *Composition (The Cow)*,
c. 1917
Pencil on paper
Sheet 4 5/8 x 6 1/4" (11.8 x 17.1 cm)
Purchase

Page 16

Henri Matisse
The Red Studio, 1911
Oil on canvas
7' 1/4"x 7' 2 1/4" (181 x 219.1 cm)
Mrs. Simon Guggenheim Fund

Matisse's interest in color could
be the main subject of this painting.
The color red dominates the work,
subverting our spatial expectations
and invading the outlined objects.